UNDERSTA
CLAS
MANAGEMENT

UNDERSTANDING CLASSROOM MANAGEMENT

An Observation Guide

Julie P. Sanford

University of Maryland, College Park

Edmund T. Emmer

University of Texas, Austin

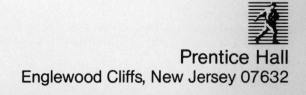

Prentice Hall
Englewood Cliffs, New Jersey 07632

Library of Congress Cataloging-in-Publication Data

Sanford, Julie P.
  Understanding classroom management.

  1. Observation (Educational method). 2. Classroom
management. 3. Teaching. 4. Teachers—Training of.
I. Emmer, Edmund T. II. Title.
LB1027.28.S26 1988   370′.7′33   87-29079
ISBN 0-13-935693-2

Cover design: Wanda Lubelska Design
Manufacturing buyer: Margaret Rizzi

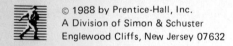 © 1988 by Prentice-Hall, Inc.
A Division of Simon & Schuster
Englewood Cliffs, New Jersey 07632

Printed in the United States of America
10 9 8 7 6 5 4 3 2 1

ISBN 0-13-935693-2   01

Prentice-Hall International (UK) Limited, *London*
Prentice-Hall of Australia Pty. Limited, *Sydney*
Prentice-Hall Canada Inc., *Toronto*
Prentice-Hall Hispanoamericana, S.A., *Mexico*
Prentice-Hall of India Private Limited, *New Delhi*
Prentice-Hall of Japan, Inc., *Tokyo*
Simon & Schuster Asia Pte. Ltd., *Singapore*
Editora Prentice-Hall do Brasil, Ltda., *Rio de Janeiro*

Contents

Preface

Observing in classrooms is an important part of learning to teach. By observing how different teachers manage their classrooms and instruct their students, you can gather useful information about a variety of ways to approach the tasks you will face as a teacher. You can also increase your understanding of the complexities of life in classrooms and of how and why teachers and students behave as they do.

Learning through observation is more efficient when you have a plan to guide your efforts. Without one you might not become aware of important aspects of classroom life or you might spend too much time focusing on elements that might not provide much insight into how classrooms operate. For example, in a truly well managed classroom it is easy to overlook the many routines and procedures the teacher uses to make the classroom run smoothly. Moreover, untrained observers sometimes focus exclusively on problem students and the teacher's reactions to them. However, such a focus is not sufficient to understand the processes that control classroom behavior. Therefore, this observation guide is designed to help you get the most out of your time and effort as you observe and analyze classrooms.

The activities in this manual focus on the important and complex topic of classroom management. Your first impression might be that this topic mainly concerns the handling of disruptive student behavior. While such teacher skills are a part of classroom management, researchers have found that effective management depends less on how teachers respond to unruly students than on how they organize classroom environments, establish procedures and routines that work, teach students what behaviors are expected, and organize activities that support student engagement in class activities. Successful management presents quite a complex set of problems, and perceiving how experienced teachers solve these problems in different classroom contexts demands time, thought, and attention to detail.

Much of the approach to classroom management featured in this book reflects not only what we have learned in our work with preservice, beginning, and experienced teachers but also the results of the program of research on classroom management we conducted at the Research and Development Center for Teacher Education at the University of Texas at Austin. That program, which concluded in 1985, was supported by the National Institute of Education.

For their willingness to field test the pilot version of this book and their valuable criticisms and advice, we thank Hilda Borko, University of Maryland at College Park; Kathy Carter, University of Arizona, Tucson; and John Smith, Goshen College, Goshen, Indiana. Finally, for her excellent assistance in manuscript preparation, we thank Eileen Banner of the Science Teaching Center, University of Maryland at College Park.

To the Instructor

This observation guide is intended for use in student teaching, in field-based courses that include classroom management, and in induction programs that allow new teachers or interns to observe other teachers. The guide's purpose is to help observers benefit from their field experiences by completing structured observation and analysis activities. Specifically, these activities are designed to increase teachers' or prospective teachers'

knowledge of classroom management concepts and terms,
understanding of the demands of the classroom setting and awareness of the details teachers must attend to in their management plans, and
ability to plan for and make decisions about management in their own classrooms.

USE OF THE GUIDE

Because this observation guide may be used in a variety of situations, it will necessarily require adaptation to the constraints and possibilities of your setting. If your observation program is an extensive one, you may wish to allow a few unstructured observations before using the guide. Otherwise, it should be used beginning with the student's first classroom observation. If the observation is conducted as part of a field-based course, use of the guide should be correlated with the classroom management content of the course.

The guide is divided into four related aspects of management: the classroom setting, classroom procedures and routines, managing student behavior, and managing instructional activities. These areas are closely related; however, it is difficult for a preservice teacher to notice and capture all of the details relevant to management at once. Having a separate guide for each area allows concentration on a particular aspect or two in each observation. Completion of all activities described in the guide will require at least five observations of a single class plus one or more interviews with the teacher. However, by combining or omitting some observation assignments, the guide can be productively adapted for use with as few as three observations. We suggest that the given sequence of topics be followed, as later observations will be more comprehensible if the observer is familiar with concepts introduced earlier.

At the elementary level, each observation ought to last at least an hour. If possible, the set of observations should be conducted at different times of the day, especially when examining Area 2 (Classroom Procedures and Routines) and Area 4 (Managing Instructional Activities), to allow the observer to see the full complement of classroom activities. At the secondary level, each observation should cover a full class period. It would also be desirable to observe the same teacher in more than one period to gain some understanding of effects of different groups of students. Likewise, observations of a second teacher would offer a valuable opportunity for comparing and contrasting behaviors, activities, and management procedures.

ASSIGNMENTS AND CLASS ACTIVITIES

The observation activities require that detailed notes be taken. Therefore, if the field experience is intended to include other activities, such as helping the teacher, conducting lessons, or tutoring students, you, your students, and their classroom teachers will need to work together to schedule the different activities. Teachers should be informed of the purpose of the observation, the need for note taking, and the types of information being collected. This is best done prior to the arrival of the observer, for it can be unnerving for a teacher to have an observer take notes, especially when the purpose is not clear.

After each observation, observers are expected to write an analysis guided by their notes and a series of questions. We have purposely specified written descriptions, rather than summary ratings or coding schemes, because the prospective teacher needs the opportunity to use the concepts in an active, generative way. Most of the guide questions are descriptive and analytic, asking the observer to explain observed events and procedures. Students should be encouraged to answer these questions fully, giving examples and interpretations of what they observed. Other questions ask observers to evaluate what they have seen, articulate their own goals, and make decisions about their future classroom practices. These written analyses also provide the instructor with a good means of assessing comprehension.

Each area of the observation guide should be accompanied by lectures and discussion activities that add details, definitions, and examples of the kinds of description and analysis students should attempt. In addition, follow-up discussions in which students compare their findings are very important because they expose students to more examples and allow comparison of alternative approaches to management problems and effects of different strategies.

PREPARING STUDENTS FOR THEIR OBSERVATIONS

The first section of the guide introduces students to the observation techniques they will use and suggests several classroom activities that provide practice in taking narrative notes and counts of student on- and off-task behavior. Field tests of this manual suggest that detailed, objective notes are important to the observation experience, enabling students to respond better to the analysis questions. Doing the suggested practice activities in class before the observation for Area 2 is attempted will be helpful. In addition, having students submit at least one set of their observation notes and questions for feedback early in their field experience is probably a good idea.

Students should be cautioned to treat the classroom observation experience in a professional manner. Points you might discuss before sending them out to observe include the following:

1. Observers should avoid being intrusive; they should not call attention to themselves or distract the students.
2. Both the teacher and the students are entitled to confidentiality. Last names should be omitted from notes, gossip should be avoided, and information that might cause embarrassment should not be revealed.
3. The observers are in classrooms as learners and should avoid making premature evaluations or conveying a critical attitude to the teacher.

The first section of the text includes additional suggestions about conduct during observations. You may wish to call special attention to the part entitled Practical Tips on Observations.

Supplemental reading in classroom management is highly desirable both to prepare the observers and to give them a framework for interpretation and evaluation. Among the number of available texts, we admit a preference for two—*Classroom Management for Secondary Teachers* (1988) by Edmund T. Emmer, Carolyn M. Evertson, Julie P. Sanford, Barbara S. Clements, and Murray E. Worsham; and *Classroom Management for Elementary Teachers* (1988) by Evertson, Emmer, Clements, Sanford, and Worsham—both published by Prentice Hall.

UNDERSTANDING CLASSROOM MANAGEMENT

Observation Techniques

This manual emphasizes not only the content of classroom management—management principles that you will see in action in your field work—but also the methods to be used in gathering and recording information about classrooms. This emphasis reflects our belief that through systematic observation you can improve your understanding of classroom organization and management.

Many different procedures have been developed for systematically observing teachers and students, including rating scales of behaviors and characteristics, checklists, counts of specific behaviors, and narrative descriptions of events and behaviors. The choice of observation procedure depends upon the purposes for the observation. For example, checklists are useful when a large number of behaviors and events must be noted in a single observation but precision is not particularly important. Rating scales are appropriate when judging the appropriateness or effectiveness of the teacher's actions. In this manual, we are concerned mainly with obtaining careful descriptions of teacher behaviors and activities in a specific area of teaching, namely management; consequently, the observation procedure that will be used most is narrative observation notes. Gathering information in this way allows you to obtain detailed information about classroom management and organization without making premature judgments about effectiveness, which might occur with rating scales.

You will also be using an observation procedure that requires obtaining frequency counts of students who are on task and off task, to assess student engagement in class activities. Student engagement is an important component of management success, and information about such engagement is useful in gauging the impact of different teacher decisions. Relying upon your memory of student behavior or narrative notes alone might not provide sufficient information about these important behaviors.

The emphasis upon descriptive accounts and specific behaviors does not mean that interpretative analysis and reflective assessment have no place in the study of classroom management. On the contrary, they are very important as you think about the type of management you will use or adapt to your own instructional style. We do, however, want to emphasize the necessity of maintaining an objective perspective as you record narrative notes of classroom events and assess student engagement, for only by preserving a faithful and unbiased record will you have an adequate basis for understanding and explaining classroom activities and drawing conclusions.

In this section, you will be introduced to several observation techniques that will be helpful in your current role as observer and student of classroom management and organization. First, definitions and guiding principles will be discussed for the two systematic observation techniques that you will use most: taking detailed observation notes and recording information about student behavior. Then we will briefly consider another way to obtain information about management—interviewing the teacher. Some practical tips and guidelines for field work will follow. Finally, we will offer exercises to give you practice with some of the techniques and concepts before you make an actual field observation.

YOUR OBSERVATION NOTES

The Importance of Observation Notes

Classrooms are fascinating places to visit. Some are like a three-ring circus, offering a great number of things to watch, including individual students, students interacting socially, teachers explaining content, students struggling with new ideas or challenging tasks, teachers dealing with disruptive students, and students helping other students. It is engaging simply to sit and watch or to interact with students. Although both of those experiences can be instructive for a student of classroom management, your field experiences are likely to be most productive if you learn to take thorough notes during observations. Note taking serves two important functions. First, the process encourages an observer to be vigilant and to notice enough details about classroom events to reach an accurate understanding not only of what happens but also of why and how. Second, good notes allow an observer to review, reflect on, and analyze events after leaving the classroom. The better your notes, the more information you will have to work with after your observation.

Guiding Principles for Observation Notes

Your observation notes are more likely to serve their intended purposes well if you follow three principles while taking them:

1. Note details and concrete examples, avoiding vague or judgmental statements.
2. Focus on the targeted behaviors for each observation.
3. Capture the general flow of events, with a balance of information about teacher and student activities.

Details and Concrete Examples

Good observation notes go beyond generalization and broad description to include many specific details and concrete examples. In several of the observation assignments in this manual you are expected to take narrative notes to record as much as possible of classroom activities. It is, of course, impossible to capture every detail about a class. However, by combining broad, general notes with specific details, quotations, and examples, you should have a rich, useful record of your observations. Means of achieving sufficient details include the following:

1. Use brief direct quotations, phrases, or specific terms rather than vague description (see Table 1).
2. Copy at least some of what the teacher writes on the blackboard or the overhead projector, especially if it relates to the area targeted for observation.
3. Try to use student's names rather than simply referring to the "students" or the "class." A seating chart is a valuable aid here. Also, listen for the teacher's use of names. If you cannot pick up the names, you might use a seating code (e.g., Student A3 means the student seated in row A, third position) or refer to some students by their outstanding characteristics (e.g., the girl in the red dress, the tallest boy).
4. Avoid interpretive and judgmental statements during the observation. Instead, try to capture objective, concrete evidence on which you can base your later interpretations. For example, "students stay interested because teacher tells them interesting facts and information" is an interpretive statement that provides little concrete information about what was observed. Recording evidence of student interest and samples of information the teacher provides is a better strategy for note taking. For example, "the teacher holds up several prints of Civil War weapons and describes the weapons' characteristics" gives more information about what the teacher did. "Three students asked questions and at least half of the class volunteered when the teacher asked a summary question" likewise provides better information about student behavior.
5. Use abbreviations and develop your own method of shorthand. Useful

TABLE 1. Examples of Descriptive Notes

Vague Description	Clearer, More Specific Notes
Teacher reprimands a boy.	T—"Jason, turn around! I said do the work on your own."
Room is pretty loud.	About half of Ss talk in low voices, others silent or whisper. Joey and Frank yell across room.
Teacher is warm and supportive.	T—"That's a great idea." T smiles. T—"You are brave to try that—I am proud of you!" T pats S on shoulder.
Andy doesn't seem to be very interested in today's lecture.	Andy folds homework paper, doodles, looks behind him, takes few notes.
Students complain a lot.	Mark—"Not fair! You didn't tell us that." Others—didn't understand directions; "Oh no!"
During lab many students just fool around.	Joey and Denise watch hamster in cage. Groups 2 and 5 talk about a party. Group 1 measuring (on task). Four students walking around aimlessly.

common abbreviations include S (student), Ss (students), T (teacher), CB (chalkboard), OP (overhead projector), and Q (question).

Focus Your Observations

Each section of this manual identifies specific aspects of management for you to observe. Questions or other assignments are provided for each area. Directing your attention and note taking during each observation toward the targeted aspects of management will help you with these postobservation assignments. Several steps will help you achieve the proper focus. First, review the terms and concepts that are defined and explained in the introduction to each area and use them as you take notes. Second, before the observation look over the questions that you will answer later. Third, during the observation refer to the list of concepts and terms in the Observation Guide for each area.

Capture the Flow of Events

In addition to noting concrete details and focusing on targeted aspects of management, you should try to describe the general flow of events to capture the overall view. Two techniques will help you do this. First, try to balance the amount of information you record about both teacher and student activities and avoid exclusively attending to the teacher or a few highly noticeable students. Be conscious of noting the students' responses to teacher directions and comments as well as the teacher's responses to student behavior. Second, make frequent notes of the time, especially when there is a change in the kind of activity (such as the beginning of a lesson or the end of a quiz), the format (how students are grouped for work), or the topic of a lesson. This will help you reconstruct the flow of events as you review your notes. Awareness of time may also help you improve your own sense of how long various classroom activities take, which is needed for instructional planning.

OBSERVING STUDENT BEHAVIOR

In several of the observation assignments in this manual you are asked to count and record students in different categories of engagement in class activities: off task, on task, and in dead time. Student engagement (that is, involvement or participation) is an important indicator of the effects or success of teachers' management decisions. Engagement counts provide clues about student use of time, cooperation, and attention during various classroom activities.

Student engagement counts are made by simply scanning the room at a specific point and counting those who appear to be off task, on task, or in dead time. Being *on task* means being appropriately engaged in whatever activity is occurring. This activity may be academic, such as writing an assignment or listening to a teacher's explanation, or it may be procedural, such as getting out supplies for the next lesson. In many cases an observer cannot know for sure whether a student is really mentally on task. The student may be daydreaming while facing the teacher or writing a letter rather than the assignment. The observer must thus simply infer that the student is on task if there is no clear sign of inappropriate behavior. Students are counted as *off task* when they are clearly *not* doing what the teacher expects them to be doing. The definition of off-task behavior depends on the rules and expectations for student behavior in each class and during different activities. Typically, off-task behaviors include talking to one's neighbor when this is not allowed, playing or socializing instead of working, being out of one's seat when this is not allowed, talking or reading inappropriate materials during a teacher's presentation, or simply not working during an assigned activity. Off-task behavior is not necessarily disruptive.

The third category of student engagement is *in dead time*, which occurs when the observer realizes that there is nothing that students are supposed to be doing. For example, a student may have finished an assignment and is simply waiting for the next activity or for the end of class. In such cases the teacher has not told students what to do, nor is there a classroom routine that establishes behavior expectations.

Usually, student engagement counts are most easily made by scanning the room for students who appear to be clearly off task and in dead time. The remaining students are assumed to be on task. When you record engagement counts, note the identities of off-task students and a word or two about their activities, if possible.

INTERVIEWING THE TEACHER

An interview with the teacher you have observed will give you several kinds of information not available through observation. First, you will be able to learn about the teacher's perspective on class events and behavior. The teacher may be able to describe prior activities or behaviors you did not have the opportunity to watch. Second, you will discover something about the teacher's planning and decision making as related to management problems, including alternatives the teacher has considered or tried in the past and reasons for the management choices the teacher has made. Third, you may ask questions to help you better understand some of the events you observed. Established routines, signals, or consequence systems may be difficult to interpret without some explanation from the teacher.

If you are using this guide during your student teaching or in another long-term arrangement, you may be able to make three or four separate interviews with the teacher, scheduling each soon after an observation. Each set of observation analysis questions in this book includes a section that requires a teacher interview. Appendix A lists suggested interview questions organized by classroom management area.

In many field settings it will be practical to interview the teacher only once. In such cases, plan to interview the teacher soon after your last observation of the class. Try to set aside at least thirty minutes for an interview in a quiet location. Before the interview, review your notes or narratives and your analyses. Select questions from Appendix A and add others as needed. If the teacher agrees, tape record your interview so that you do not have to take notes and can review the tape later to summarize the teacher's responses.

PRACTICAL TIPS ON OBSERVATIONS

Several practical tips can make your field observations go more smoothly and successfully. Some that pertain directly to the assignments in this manual are listed below.

What to Tell the Teacher

It is important to build rapport with the observed teacher so that he feels comfortable with your presence in his classroom and with your systematic observation and note taking. Think how you might feel if a stranger entered *your* classroom and began writing copious notes as *you* taught! It is important that you introduce yourself in a friendly, courteous manner and that you let the teacher know that you are there to learn and observe. Avoid projecting a judgmental or evaluative attitude.

Before your first observation, contact the teacher to confirm your appointment time and place and agree on a schedule for your observations. With regard to the observation assignments contained in this manual, you may wish to tell the teacher the following:

1. Your assignments are designed to help you gather as much information as possible about organization and management of different kinds of classroom activities. You will be focusing on classroom procedures and routines, management of student behavior, and organization of instructional activities.
2. You are supposed to take detailed notes during class to help you remember and reflect on what you saw and respond to exercise questions. Therefore, for at least some of your observations (depending on how many of the assignments in this manual are attempted) you will need to observe and take notes rather than interact with students.
3. You would like to interview the teacher sometime after your observations to hear the teacher's perspective on planning and management. (Arrange for a time convenient for the teacher and sufficient to answer the questions you wish to ask.)

If your field experience is supposed to include activities other than those described in this guide (such as tutoring, working with small groups, or serving as an aide), be sure to reach an understanding with the teacher about schedules for the different activities.

Preparing for the Observations

It is a good idea to make a trip to the school before your first observation to find out how to get there, where to park, how long travel will take, and where the office and your assigned classroom are. If you cannot make an advance "scouting" trip, give yourself plenty of time before your first appointment with the teacher to avoid being late. On arrival, check in at the office and find out what sign-in procedures you will be expected to follow. Dress in a conservative, professional manner. A good guideline is to try to look like the other teachers in the school.

For each observation, bring plenty of paper, an extra pencil, and a watch. Arrive at your classroom before the students do. Ask the teacher where she would like you to sit so that you will not be distracting or in the way but can see and hear well. Either borrow a seating chart from the teacher or make one and fill in the students' names as you learn them.

Behavior During the Observations

During the observations try to be unobtrusive. It is usually best not to move around the classroom except during major activity changes or group work, when your movements are less likely to be distracting. It is generally a good idea to avoid eye contact with students while you are observing. If students speak to you, act pleasant but preoccupied with your work.

Behavior After the Observations

At the end of the observations, if it is convenient for the teacher, let him know that you enjoyed and appreciated the opportunity to watch the class. Do not, however, expect the teacher to give you attention at that time if you have not made an appointment. Soon after leaving the class, review your notes and fill in any blanks or unreadable places. Respond to the analysis questions or other assignments soon thereafter, while your memory is fresh.

PREOBSERVATION EXERCISES

1. Figure 1 is an excerpt from narrative notes taken during a seventh-grade English class. As you read the excerpt, consider the amount, kind, and quality of information the observer has captured. Then discuss the following questions:

    1. Did the narrative provide enough information to give you a clear picture of class events?
    2. About what aspects of the class did the narrative contain the most information? About what aspects is there less information?
    3. What information is given about the behavior and activities of students as a group? As individuals? How are individual students identified?
    4. Where did the observer provide concrete examples or quotations? Where did the observer summarize or make broad statements?
    5. What observer biases or interpretations, if any, are evident?

Mrs. Brown, English, Grade 7, Period 1   Tues.; Oct. 7

Time	
8:45	Desks in rows face front board. T desk at back of room, behind Ss. Lots of student work on bulletin boards. 24 Ss are in the room and seated when the bell rings. T talks to one student at his desk near front, then she begins class by reminding Ss that she doesn't accept late work. Urges them to get work in on time. T smiles, sounds firm but encouraging. T tells Ss to get out notes from yesterday. they do. 2 girls talk. T - quietly - "There should be no talking now." Girls get quiet. T writes title and date on board and answers one boy's question, then begins a lesson on nouns, possessive forms. T asks a question, calls on Mark, who doesn't know. T - "Okay. Can anyone else think of any?" 4-5 volunteers raise hands. Lesson goes on. Most Ss pay attention; many volunteers.
8:50	2 girls OFF TASK at back corner, whispering. T ignores, calls on different Ss to answer questions, and also presents new material, tells Ss to take notes she writes on board. T asks Jolene to get rid of gum in back trash, and she does without comment.
8:52	T now tells the class to copy one paragraph from their book: "The reason is we are learning two characteristics of nouns." T states characteristics (you can make a noun show possession by adding 's or '). T repeats, explains.

FIGURE 1. Excerpts from Narrative Notes

Mrs. Brown, English, Grade 7, Period 1   *Tues.; Oct. 7*

Time	
8:54	All Ss seem to copy. T goes back to her desk and checks roll silently. Ss completely quiet, work. One girl raises hand. The T goes to student's desk and answers her question.
8:55	Most Ss still write, but T says they should be just about through. She waits, standing near Steve at front, and watches. "Look on p. 20." She reads a sentence aloud, tells Ss to find it. She waits, repeats. Copy these 2 sentences about making nouns plural. Repeats again. Ss copy. T helps Karen find place, catch up. This quietly at S's desk. T smiles. T waits, then restates 2 things that distinguish nouns – ways of forming plural and possessive. Some Ss still write.
8:59	T– "What I would do if these were my notes and if I were studying for a test on nouns is:" T shows on board how she would mark most important things with an * and how she would label topics in the margin. T repeats most important facts, makes objectives very clear.
9:00	No Ss OFF TASK. Most look at T. Some write.
9:02	T begins to call on Ss, going down rows, to answer questions in exercise in textbook. Most students can do it. T "Good" "You've got this well." Danny doesn't know the meaning of a word. T defines it. Jolene can't answer. T reads question for her, waits "You know that!... Good!"

FIGURE 1 (continued)

Time	Mrs. Brown, English, Grade 7, Period 1 Tues.; Oct. 7
9:05	End of exercise. T announces library. Asks Ss who have checked out books if they brought them. 4 Ss (includes Danny, Joe) who forgot books raise hands. T - "I warned you! What can I do? Bring tomorrow." Discussion of library rules about checking out only 2 books.
9:07	Jolene and other girl OFF TASK, talking. T ignores. Others get louder as move to door. T tells class to whisper on way to library, not to go to restroom or get water. She says they have only 10 minutes. No socializing. Steve calls out, joking about socializing. T - "If you don't realize the purpose of library, you can stay in Mr. Ham's room!" He gets quiet. They leave.

FIGURE 1 (continued)

2. Observe a videotape of a class session, preferably one that shows both teacher and student activities. Take narrative notes of a segment of fifteen to twenty minutes, trying to record as much as you can of the events and the setting. (Warning: Practicing observation techniques using a videotape can be more difficult than field observation. Do not become discouraged in your first efforts.) Compare your notes with those of other class members. How do they vary in their focus, the amount of detail, specificity, and objectivity?

3. In class or with a partner, practice making decisions about student on-task, off-task, and dead-time behavior by watching a classroom teaching videotape in which a number of students are on camera at least part of the time. At selected times when students are on camera, use the pause button to freeze frame just long enough to determine which students are on task, which are off task, and which are in dead time. Record your results and some brief notes as in the example on the next page:

Pause	Off Task	Dead Time	On Task
Pause 1	2—Mary and other girl at door	—	6
Pause 2	—	4—Group 1 waiting for teacher	4
Pause 3	1—Boy, right corner on floor	—	8

After this exercise, rerun the tape and, with your classmates or partner, compare and discuss your student engagement counts.

4. As an alternative or supplement to Exercises 2 and 3, use role playing to provide observation practice. Divide the class into two groups and have someone lead an instructional activity with one group while the remainder of the class practices taking observation notes. At various times, some "students" can become off task to provide practice in assessing student engagement. Switch student and observer roles so that everyone has a chance to practice. Compare notes and counts, as above.

Your name _____ **Date** _____

Class observed and grade _____

YOUR OBSERVATION SETTING

After your initial visit to the classroom you will be observing, outline the *context* of your field observation by describing the community setting, the school, the grade, the designated level and subject (if appropriate), and the class composition. You can add to this description later as you learn more about the class.

AREA 1
The Classroom Setting

Your observation and study of classroom management will begin with a close look at how the classroom itself is organized. This is a logical place to start because the room's physical arrangements affect student behavior and can make managing a class an easier or more difficult task. Understanding these influences, therefore, is an important part of learning how classrooms work. Another reason for examining the setting is to avoid viewing it as fixed and unchangeable. To an observer, alternatives to a classroom's arrangement might not be easily imagined. By analyzing the room's features and comparing it with other rooms, you can envision other arrangements and purposes they might serve. Finally, you should remember that you will eventually need to create a working classroom out of four walls, thirty desks, and a lot of equipment and materials. You will be better equipped for that task if you begin to look for helpful features and to notice potential problems now.

IMPORTANT CONCEPTS FOR THIS OBSERVATION

A good start toward understanding how a room's physical features contribute to classroom management is to notice what equipment and furniture are used in teaching and how they are arranged. Some of the most common elements are

the teacher's and students' desks
other furniture
walls, windows, and doors
chalkboards
bulletin boards and other displays
overhead projector and screen
pencil sharpener and waste bins
work areas
supply and storage areas
special equipment

In the observation guide for this chapter, you will be asked to prepare a sketch of the classroom that shows these and other salient features.

As you observe the students and the teacher using the room, note how various parts of the room are used in different activities, especially in frequent ones such as whole class presentations, seat work, and small group instruction. The following key concepts and principles will help make your observations and analysis of the physical setting fruitful.

Student Seating Arrangement

The student seating arrangement is an important feature of the classroom. In addition to the common row and aisle pattern, many other arrangements can be found, including desks in two facing groups, separated by an aisle; tables rather than desks (note how students store books and other materials); a semicircular pattern; and clusters of four to six desks. Consider the advantages the various arrangements may have for the teacher and students. For example, frequent teacher presentations to the whole class will make a traditional seating arrangement (rows of desks facing forward) functional, whereas frequent use of cooperative student work groups would make clusters of desks desirable. You may not be able to judge functionality after a single observation, and an interview with the teacher may reveal other reasons for a particular seating arrangement. In addition to the overall arrangement, see if you can identify where students who seem to need extra teacher attention or assistance are located.

Traffic Patterns

Traffic patterns, or common routes for teacher and student movement about the room, should be noted, along with student entrances and exits from the room. Congestion sometimes occurs at such high-use areas as the pencil sharpener, the teacher's desk, the door, and frequently used supply shelves, and students seated near these areas may be distracted from their work. Such frequently used routes should be unobstructed, and materials that are often used need to be easily accessible.

Visibility for the Teacher

Another important principle is that the teacher should be able to observe all students at all times because close monitoring allows the teacher to detect problems early and to take prompt action. The classroom arrangement can affect teacher monitoring capability, for in certain arrangements some students may not be easily observed. For example, a bookshelf or room partition may block the teacher's view of students using a reading corner or learning center.

During teacher presentations to the whole class, note whether the location of the teacher and equipment (for example, an overhead projector or chart stand) permit easy observation of all students. If the teacher conducts small group activities during your observation, notice both the placement of the small group in relation to the rest of the class and the teacher's position in the small group. Which students or room areas are relatively difficult for the teacher to see? What alternative arrangements are possible? If students work at centers or in special areas for certain activities, observe whether the teacher moves around the room or stays in one or two areas and if the students can easily be monitored.

Visibility for Students

Visibility for students is, of course, equally important. Can students easily see the chalkboard or the overhead projector screen? Do they have to turn around or dodge other students to see? Are distracting displays (e.g., a gerbil cage) or open windows in their line of vision? In certain seating arrangements some students have their backs to the main instructional area and must turn around to see. Even when seated in rows facing forward, students at the periphery may have difficulty seeing. In the classroom you are observing, consider what visibility problems exist and how they might be alleviated.

Classroom Ambience

The general appearance, organization, and maintenance of a room contribute to the classroom ambience. Arrangements of furniture, materials, and displays may communicate a sense of order and efficiency or of confusion and lack of care. Displays may reflect a conscious effort by the teacher to stimulate students' interests, creativity, and enthusiasm, or they may support important affective, social, or managerial goals. Neat displays of students' work, assignment schedules, and reminders of work requirements may underline the value placed on academic goals and conscientious effort. As you observe, consider the overall effect of the classroom's appearance on its climate. Note displays, decorations, posted rules, and maintenance. What aspects of classroom management or instruction are supported, and what values are emphasized?

Finally, teachers often must accommodate their classroom organization to constraints such as too little space, poor lighting, limited chalkboard, storage, or display space, awkwardly placed electrical outlets or windows, and inadequate equipment. Identify any such factors that appear to be important influences in the classroom you are observing.

OBSERVATION GUIDE 1.   The Classroom Setting

ACTIVITY 1.1.   Room Diagram

Prepare a sketch of the classroom you are observing. Try to retain proportionality among objects and dimensions, and show such features as furniture, walls, windows, doors, displays, overhead projector, pencil sharpener, wastebasket, equipment, supplies, and storage.

ACTIVITY 1.2.   Observing the Physical Setting

During an observation, take notes about the following features of the room and types of classroom activities that you observe:

Displays

Information about rules, grading,
   community and school events, etc.
Student work
Assignments and due dates

Teacher Monitoring at or from

Whole class presentation areas
Administrative business areas
Small group meeting place
Low visibility areas (if any)

Traffic Patterns to or Around

Entrance to the room
Students' desks and aisles
Teacher's desk
Work, supply, and storage areas
Pencil sharpener
Wastebaskets
Water fountain
Restrooms

Other Aspects

General appearance and ambience
Student visibility
Constraints and their accommodation
Places for turning in or picking up
   work

Your name _____ Date _____

Class observed and grade _____

ACTIVITY 1.3. Observation Analysis Questions

Answer the following questions as soon as possible after your observation. Use your classroom sketch and your notes as memory aids.

1. Describe the general arrangement of furniture and work space (or attach a room diagram) and indicate the general appearance of the room.

2. Describe major traffic patterns in the room, including any related problems, such as crowding or distractions.

3. When arranging the classroom, how did the teacher deal with any physical constraints, such as a small room, inadequate chalkboard space, or special equipment?

4. Describe student seating arrangements and whether they changed depending on the activity. Where were the students who seemed to need special attention or assistance?

5. How did the teacher provide space for small group work or teacher-student conferences or tutoring?

6. Could students see instructional displays and activities? Could all students be easily seen by the teacher at all times?

7. What values or goals were emphasized or supported by the overall appearance of the room? Explain your answer by describing the displays, decorations, and other aspects that affected the classroom climate.

8. Which aspects of the room arrangement you observed would you retain and which would you alter? Consider the seating arrangements, traffic patterns, work and storage areas, teacher monitoring and student visibility, and general room appearance. Indicate your reasons for your decision.

ACTIVITY 1.4. Further Questions

If you have had the opportunity to interview the teacher about the classroom setting (see Appendix A for suggested interview questions), the following questions can be answered:

1. What aspects of this classroom setting did the teacher mention as important or problematic?

2. Describe the teacher's policy or procedures for determining student seating arrangements. How often are arrangements changed, and what changes have been made since the beginning of the year?

3. What procedures does the teacher use for keeping papers for different classes or subject areas organized and separated?

4. Comment on any additional information you learned about classroom arrangement and organization from your interview.

AREA 2

Classroom Procedures and Routines

Good classroom management requires that routine business, such as checking the roll, passing papers, dealing with tardy students, and beginning and ending class, be handled efficiently. Good management also requires procedures for instruction that maintain the proper academic focus and make appropriate use of time. Therefore, teachers need to develop supporting routines that govern the students' talk, movement, and work. Such routines allow the teacher and students to concentrate on learning and help prevent inappropriate behavior.

The goals for management in the area of classroom procedures, routines, and rules is to establish a set of expectations that guide student behavior at different times and in various activities. This system of procedures and routines should support an efficient, pleasant, task-focused classroom climate and minimize the time and effort devoted to noninstructional matters.

Which set of routines and procedures is best? The answer will vary from class to class, for there is no one best way to run all elementary or secondary classes. The teacher's goals and the types of students will affect the management system and the amount of attention that must be devoted to establishing classroom procedures and routines. It *is* true, however, that to organize and manage a classroom, you will need to develop a set of procedures and rules that work for you and your students and that support academic instruction. If you do not do so, you may have to struggle daily—perhaps constantly—with routine matters such as movement about the room, whether and when students must raise their hands to speak, and how to turn papers in. Furthermore, to establish workable procedures, you must formulate them in advance, teach them to the students, and use them consistently. By observing procedures and routines now, you will begin to develop your ideas about what will work for you and what will be consistent with your goals for your students.

IMPORTANT CONCEPTS FOR THIS OBSERVATION

The purpose of this observation is to identify and analyze the procedures and routines that govern behavior in your observation classroom. The observation guide calls attention to five major areas of procedures and describes what to watch for and think about in each area. You may not be able to gather complete information about each area during a single observation; however, prior observations that you may have made in the same class and an interview with the teacher may help you answer the questions that follow the guide.

Administrative Routines

In elementary classrooms, the beginning of the day is often accompanied by whole class routines such as a song, the Pledge of Allegiance, and announcements. Teachers also often handle administrative matters such as attendance checks and milk and lunch counts at this time. End-of-day procedures may include cleaning up, conducting whole class discussions of the day's events, distributing materials to be taken home, and giving reminders for the next day.

Secondary teachers, with several classes per day, will often have a shorter opening than their elementary counterparts. Some may engage students in a warm-up (a short seat-work review assignment), and most will have some routine for handling attendance checks, tardy students, and other administrative matters.

When you observe, note what both the teacher and the students do during the beginning and ending activities. What administrative matters are handled then and at other times? How are tardy and previously absent students dealt with? What attendance checking process is used?

Procedures for Student Talk and Movement

This area of management needs to be very carefully considered, because inappropriate student talk and movement are very common problems encountered by teachers at all grade levels. In most situations teaching is just plain difficult if students are constantly chattering and wandering around the room!

Expectations for student talk vary depending on the activity. During whole-class, teacher-led instruction, a common expectation is for students to raise their hands and wait to be called on before speaking. Some teachers, however, may encourage "call outs" or choral responding in specific situations. For seat-work activities, teacher expectations vary more: Some teachers permit quiet talking among students, while others permit none. Be sure to note what procedures are in place during your observation and how they are differentiated across activities. Check for posted rules about talk and movement, and note the circumstances under which the teacher corrects student behavior. Note also how students obtain assistance during seat work.

Expectations for student movement around the room may also be a function of the nature of the class activity. Note the circumstances under which students are permitted to leave their seats and whether there is any limitation, such as the number of students permitted to move, where they may go, what they may do, and whether the teacher's explicit permission is required. Also, if students leave the room, note the circumstances and expectations for their behavior.

Procedures for Managing Student Work

A classroom is a busy place, with students working on an assortment of assignments, exercises, and projects. Many student products are generated by these activities, so procedures are needed for handling this work. During your observation, note how each assignment is communicated to the students and whether it is posted on a bulletin board or a chalkboard. What are the teacher's expectations for student products, and how are these expectations communicated? Determine the teacher's system for collecting and returning assignments. If students help by grading their own or others' work in class, what procedures contribute to the efficiency and accuracy of this checking? If students finish assignments early, what are they expected to do? Finally, procedures for handling absent students' work should be noted: How do these students find out what work they missed? How much time do they have to complete such work? How can help be obtained, if needed?

Procedures for Student Use of Equipment and Supplies

Determine which equipment and supplies are used during your observation. Some things will be standard, such as pencil sharpener, wastebaskets, bookshelves, desks, and tables. Many rooms will also have audiovisual equipment, computers, microscopes, sinks, and the like. Some areas of the room may be set aside for work centers, displays, or other special use. Generally, specific procedures will govern the time and duration of their use and general student conduct.

Procedures for Group Work

Although aspects of group work procedures have been discussed, the use of special groups is sufficiently complex to warrant separate consideration. Two types of group work are commonly used. One type, frequently found in elementary schools, is the small, teacher-led group, usually employed for reading or language arts instruction and sometimes during mathematics. During group time the students not receiving instruction from the teacher are generally occupied with seat-work activities. Especially critical expectations are those governing student talk (in and out of the group), student movement, and how students in seatwork obtain assistance. A second type of group work is the independent work group, in which group members work on a common assignment, project, or laboratory exercise. Important considerations include the teacher's monitoring of student progress and behavior, the clarity of directions, the procedures that govern student talk, movement, and roles, and the use of equipment and supplies. In laboratory settings, procedures for the use of complex equipment and potentially dangerous materials are also crucial. Make careful note of safety procedures and how they are communicated to students.

OBSERVATION GUIDE 2.   Classroom Procedures and Routines

ACTIVITY 2.1.   Observe and Take Notes

Before the observation review your notes from Area 1 about room displays or other evidence of procedures in the room, such as posted rules; lists, reminders, or notes regarding consequences or routines; lists of student helpers or class officers; and calendars of weekly or daily events. During your observation, focus on the routines, procedures, and rules that seem to be governing students' behavior and activities. If the class appears to proceed smoothly with few statements by the teacher about behavior, try to infer the expectations or standards from actions. In general, try to capture some information about the following:

Beginning and Ending of Class

What the teacher does
What the students do
Attendance check
Dealing with tardy students
Money collection
Other administrative routines

*Student Use of Equipment
and Supplies*

Pencil sharpener
Wastebasket
Desks
Supply shelves
Storage areas
Sink and water fountain
Special equipment

Student Talk and Movement

During lessons
During seat work
Between activities
When students need help
Entering and leaving the room

Group Work Procedures

Expectations for student talk and
   movement
Teacher monitoring of student
   progress
Use of equipment and supplies
Directions to students

Managing Student Work

Giving assignments
Criteria for work
Procedures for absent students
Collecting, grading, and returning
   work
What students do when they com-
   plete assignments early

Your name _____ **Date** _____

Class observed and grade _____

ACTIVITY 2.2. Observation Analysis Questions

Using your class notes, answer the following questions as soon as possible after your observation:

1. Describe the procedures or policies that governed behavior in each of the five major areas listed in Activity 2.1. Use additional paper if you need more space.

2. For each of the five areas listed above, discuss how well the teacher's procedures contributed to the conduct of instructional activities and the efficient use of time. If you noted especially helpful procedures or if problems occurred in some area, describe what happened.

3. When you have your own classroom, what procedures have you observed that you are likely to use without change? Which would you adapt and how? Which would you not use and why not?

ACTIVITY 2.3.   Further Questions

If you have had the opportunity to interview your teacher about classroom procedures and routines (see Appendix A for suggested interview questions), the following questions can be answered:

1.   Describe how your teacher developed or came to use the classroom procedures you observed, especially those in the five areas listed in Activity 2.1.

2.   How did your teacher explain expected behavior to the students at the beginning of the year or at other times?

3.   What changes, if any, have been made in rules or routines during the year and why?

4.   What routines or procedures did the teacher describe as particularly important or difficult to deal with? What specific recommendations would this teacher make to a beginning teacher?

AREA 3
Managing Student Behavior

Even a well-designed set of classroom procedures, rules, and routines will not be effective for long if a teacher cannot maintain students' involvement and prevent disruption of instructional activities. Furthermore, it would be a rare class in which students never misbehaved; consequently, teachers need to be prepared to handle problems when they do arise. The guide for Area 3 will help you understand how teachers keep students engaged in activities and how they deal with uncooperative or disruptive student behavior.

Probably the first association people make when they consider the concept "managing student behavior" is handling problem situations, such as dealing with a disruptive student or stopping widespread misbehavior. Effective response to such situations is indeed one part of good management. However, we should also emphasize a second facet, which research has identified as important: the *prevention* of problems through strategies and behaviors that increase student involvement in class activities and lessen the degree to which teachers must deal with misbehavior.

In keeping with the dual emphasis on effective response and prevention, Area 3 is divided into two parts. The first discusses ways of dealing with problem behaviors in the classroom; the second examines strategies for keeping students engaged in classroom activities and thereby minimizing or preventing behavior problems. The Observation Guide will ask you to look for specific student behaviors that might be labeled problems and to describe how they were handled. In addition, you will note preventive strategies used by the teacher.

MANAGING PROBLEM BEHAVIORS

There are different types of student behaviors that might be labeled as problems. One type is transitory and minor inattention, such as looking around, daydreaming, playing, or whispering. A second class of behavior is extended off-task behavior. This is similar to the first category, except that it lasts longer and has more potential to interfere with class activities. Examples include loud talking, extended conversation among several students, teasing, passing notes, out-of-seat movement, and persistent inattention. A third type of problem behavior is disruption or interference with the teacher's instruction or with other students' activities. Examples include defiance of class rules or the teacher's requests, hitting and other forms of aggression, and persistent noisiness and other forms of interference with students' rights to work and participate in class activities.

How much of these three kinds of behaviors you will observe depends on many factors, including the age and grade level of the students, the type of class and school, the individual students, the teacher's ability to limit inappropriate behavior, and the particular activities you observe. Also, it is important to remember that teachers vary in their tolerance for certain behaviors. However, in spite of differences among teachers and students, the three classes of problem behavior are worth distinguishing because the strategies for dealing with them are usually quite different.

COMMON STRATEGIES FOR RESPONDING TO STUDENT BEHAVIOR

Teacher strategies for dealing with student behavior range from no reaction to major interventions requiring extensive time and effort. This range is described below, followed by a discussion of when the various strategies are most likely to be used.

Limited Interventions

Many teacher strategies for responding to student misbehavior are very brief and may not be apparent to a casual observer. Frequently, these momentary reactions occur when the teacher's and students' attention is focused on a lesson or assignment that the teacher does not want interrupted.

Ignoring

The teacher makes no response to the student and does nothing to call attention to the student's behavior.

Physical Proximity

The teacher moves closer to the student engaged in the inappropriate behavior. This may occur as the teacher presents information or asks questions or during seat work and other activities.

Eye Contact

The teacher looks at the student until eye contact is made and the inappropriate behavior ceases. As with proximity control, eye contact can be made without interrupting an ongoing activity.

Redirection

This strategy simply involves indicating what the student is supposed to be doing. It can take the form of giving a direction to an off-task student ("This is the time for heading your spelling paper.") or a reminder or hint of what is expected ("Everyone is supposed to be finishing page nineteen now."). In the lower grades, teachers will sometimes redirect students by praising the desired appropriate behavior ("I like the way so many students are working carefully on their maps.").

Desist Statements

Sometimes students just need to be told to stop misbehaving with a desist statement such as "Please put that away and look up here." Sometimes desist statements are issued as questions that help call attention to the correct behavior: "What are you supposed to be doing now?" or "Do we talk when someone else is speaking?'' These statements are often accompanied by eye contact to communicate that the teacher means business and to identify the target of the comment.

These teacher strategies, which range from nonintervention (ignoring) to relatively brief, simple statements, are often used to deal with two types of misbehavior: inattention and off-task behavior. Two key principles underlie the teacher's response to these behaviors and make these simple strategies useful in dealing with them:

1. *Avoid interruptions to activity.* Interruptions include anything that distracts student attention from the task. Once an activity is interrupted, the teacher must reengage the class, and during the interruption there is always the potential for more students to become inattentive or off-task. Consequently, the most desirable strategies permit the teacher to manage the student behavior without intruding into the ongoing activity.

2. *Inappropriate behavior should be promptly stopped.* Off-task behavior (e.g., inappropriate talking during a presentation) that is allowed to persist may soon spread to other students and even to a large segment of the class. Other kinds of inappropriate behavior, such as teasing, can intensify and lead to more disruptive events. When this form of behavior spreads or intensifies, it is more difficult to deal with and almost certainly interrupts class activities; it may also elicit persistent and nonproductive behavior patterns.

The teacher faces a complex problem when applying these two principles, for if inappropriate behavior is ignored, the teacher risks escalation to a more serious problem; however, if the teacher intervenes to stop the behavior, class activity may be interrupted, and frequent interruptions may produce high rates of inattention or other inappropriate behavior. Teachers must make many such difficult decisions each day.

When you observe, you will need to note the types of student behaviors and the teacher's responses to them. Most teachers will ignore transient student inattention and minor off-task behaviors such as daydreaming or looking around, responding to them only when they persist. When these and other such behaviors do persist, you will need to note whether the teacher chooses to deal with them by proximity, eye contact, redirection, desist statements, or other strategies described below. It will also be important to note how successfully these strategies simultaneously deal with the problem and maintain the flow of activity. What factors—perhaps the promptness of the teacher's action or the cooperation of the students—contributed to the success of the intervention? What other approaches could be used?

Major Interventions

In addition to the strategies described above, several other options can be exercised when dealing with inappropriate behavior. These strategies are labeled "major" because they often are of longer duration, more intense, and more likely to interrupt other class activities. They are also more likely to involve some form of punishment.

Isolation or Removal of Students

A disruptive student can be moved to an area of the room where she is less likely to engage in inappropriate behavior. This is an especially common strategy when the problem involves several students seated together. Sometimes students are also temporarily removed from the room and must wait in the hallway or go to the school office.

Criticism

Teachers sometimes direct criticism at the offending behavior or, less desirably, at the student. Criticism may be conveyed through the teacher's words, tone, facial features, and other body language.

Description of the Problem

Another verbal strategy is for the teacher to describe the problem and call for or imply the need for a change in behavior. For example, if student conversation during seat work is excessive, the teacher might state: "It's so noisy in here I can't concentrate, and neither can some of you." Or a teacher might call students' attention to a rule or procedure that is not being followed: "A lot of people are forgetting how we participate in discussions. Who remembers what you need to do before you talk?" One purpose of this strategy is to increase the students' sense of responsibility for their behavior. Instead of the teacher telling them what to do, the student is being offered the opportunity for self-correction.

Strong Desist Statements

This is just a desist statement issued in a very emphatic tone ("You need to stop that behavior *now*!") and accompanied by the maintenance of eye contact and other body language that intensely conveys that the teacher means business.

Checks or Demerits

The teacher may use a system in which the accumulation of checks or demerits for problem behavior results in a specific penalty. For example, a teacher may write an offending student's name on the chalkboard and add a check after subsequent misbehavior. A certain number of checks results in specific penalties, such as detention. When observing such a system, note how frequently it is used, the types of behaviors that warrant a demerit, and whether it gives undue attention to misbehavior.

Specific Prescribed Consequences

The teacher may also decide that particular forms of misbehavior will result in punishment prescribed by school or class rules; for example, tardiness may result in detention, fighting may result in suspension.

Logical Consequences

Teachers may tailor the consequences of inappropriate behavior to its circumstances. Thus students who run in the hallway might be told to "return to go" and walk; students who talk too loudly during group projects can lose the privilege of working with the group; and students who fail to finish their assignments because they wasted time might be told to remain in the room during recess or after school until the work is completed.

Individual Conference with the Student

This approach would typically be used outside of class, although teachers sometimes privately conduct conferences during class while other students are working. During a conference, the teacher may ask the student to describe the problem from his perspective or simply state what the problem is and insist that the student accept responsibility for it. Often there is an emphasis on obtaining a commitment from the student to change the behavior.

A major intervention is most commonly used with the most severe class of problem behaviors because students who have become really disruptive may not easily be brought back into compliance by simple interventions such as a reminder or eye contact. However, major interventions are sometimes used for lesser misbehaviors as well. Often the classroom context will influence the teacher's choice of when and how to intervene. For example, during a whole class discussion, teachers may be more likely to respond quickly to inappropriate student talk and use a limited intervention; however, during a seat-work assignment, the teacher might ignore talk longer. (These differences associated with activity formats are examined further in Area 4.) Likewise, a teacher's reaction may be influenced by whether the behavior has occurred for the first time or for the nth time.

Disruptive behavior is the least common of the three classes of classroom behavior problems, so major interventions are less likely to be observed than the simpler, less intrusive ones. For this reason, you may not have an opportunity to observe how the teacher handles disruptive behavior, and you may have to depend on an interview for this information.

PREVENTIVE STRATEGIES

The preceding sections have emphasized the teacher's response to problem behaviors. It is also very important to note how the teacher *prevents* such behaviors, because it is easier and more productive to encourage and maintain appropriate behavior than it is to deal with misbehavior.

Preventive strategies are those actions teachers take before inappropriate or disruptive behavior occurs. To a degree, any teacher action that engages students in class activities can be regarded as preventive, because students will be much less likely to engage in inappropriate behavior if they are involved in a constructive activity. Some of these general preventive strategies involve arranging the physical setting (see Area 1), establishing expectations for behavior (see Area 2), and managing instructional activities (see Area 4).

Although they all contribute to preventive management, they will not be reiterated in the Observation Guide for Area 3. Instead, we will examine a more limited set of strategies: monitoring, a smooth activity flow, consistency, and incentives.

Teacher Monitoring

Awareness of what is occurring in the classroom is quite important to prevention, because an alert teacher is able to assist students who encounter difficulty with assignments and other tasks and to direct student behavior along constructive paths and away from trouble. Students soon learn whether a teacher is keeping track of their behavior; most take fewer liberties with good monitors. Good monitoring has several components, including visual scanning and frequent movement around the room. Good monitors will also have systematic processes for keeping track of student work in progress and at completion. When you are observing, look for the following indications of teacher monitoring:

1. Looking around the class at all students, rather than just at those nearby.
2. Walking around the room during seat work and checking individual student progress.
3. Giving brief (rather than extended) assistance to individual students before moving on to assist other students.
4. Maintaining eye contact with students during presentations instead of looking mainly at the chalkboard, notes, or overhead transparency.

A Smooth Activity Flow

Research by Kounin[1] and others indicated that an essential feature of good management is the ability to keep classroom activities moving without frequent interruptions. Effective managers protect their activities from both external and internal interruptions and thus are better able to maintain student attention and involvement in lessons.

There are many ways in which teachers can work toward a smooth activity flow; for example, they can handle minor problems such as inattentiveness unobtrusively rather than by stopping the lesson. Other aspects of this technique to watch for, in addition to those covered in other sections of this Observation Guide, include the following:

1. Orderly and clear presentations of information and directions. Students who understand explanations of content and know what to do when working on assignments or projects are less likely to interrupt lessons. Look for the use of step-by-step instructions, visual aids, outlines, and easy-to-follow explanations.
2. Efficient transitions from one activity to the next, such as from a whole group presentation to small group instruction or seatwork. Transitions

---

[1] J. S. Kounin, *Discipline and Group Management in Classrooms* (New York: Holt, Rinehart, and Winston, 1970).

are usually most efficient when the teacher signals or announces the beginning of a transition, monitors students during the transition, and begins the next activity promptly.

3. Maintaining a brisk but not hurried pace during instruction. If a teacher slows down a presentation student attention tends to wane. Watch for lessons and presentations in which the teacher moves on to the next point or component before student attention wanders.

Consistency

When students know that the teacher's expectations for behavior are consistent, there is a better chance of achieving good discipline. Students are less prone to test such a system to determine its limits, and the teacher is able to spend more time instructing and less time explaining correct behavior. Consistency is especially important in using class and school rules, major procedures, and instructional routines. Pay special attention to whether behavior expectations are consistent for frequent activities. For example, note procedures for student talk and movement during seat work. Do students seem to know and to follow the same guidelines at different times? If the teacher sometimes allows students to talk or to move around while at other times such behavior is forbidden, what appears to be the reason for such variation? How does the teacher signal changes in expectations? What appear to be the effects of such variations?

Consistency is also fostered by the use of a schedule and routine for activities. Thus, in elementary grades, look for a schedule of subjects and a routine for beginning and ending the day or for leaving and entering the room. At the secondary level, note how the period begins and ends and whether established procedures govern behavior at those times.

Some aspects of consistency cannot be assessed during a single observation. However, if you have observed the same classroom on several occasions, you may be able to recall certain expectations and routines that have either remained constant or changed. Take note of such areas and try to add to your store of information during future visits.

Incentives

Incentives for proper student behavior and work also play a role in preventing misbehavior. Teachers may establish incentives for performance and participation, in addition to the use of grades. Note whether any of the following are so used:

Displays of student work

Charts or lists showing student progress or completed tasks

Bonus points or extra credit

Free time or time for engaging in favorite activities

Treats, parties, or other food incentives

Honor students, notes of praise sent home, certificates, or other forms of recognition

Tokens, checks, or other symbols that can be accumulated and redeemed for prizes or privileges

If you observe one or more of these incentives, note what must be done to earn the reward and how many students receive it. Is the incentive an integral part of the classroom or is it a supplement that is used sparingly or with a limited number of students?

OBSERVATION GUIDE 3. Managing Student Behavior

ACTIVITY 3.1. Observe and Take Notes

Take detailed narrative notes of the class, focusing on student behavior, teacher responses to problems, and preventive strategies. Scan the room frequently, evaluating the degree to which students are engaged in class activities and noting examples of the categories of student behavior and teacher strategies outlined below.

Student Behaviors	*Teacher Strategies*
Inattention (e.g., looking around, daydreaming, or brief whispering)	Responses to student behavior
	Limited interventions
	Major interventions
Off-task behavior (e.g., persistent inattention, talking. or being out of seat at inappropriate times)	Preventive strategies
	Monitoring
Disruption (e.g., interfering with the teacher or other students' work)	Smooth activity flow
	Consistency
	Incentives

Your name _____ Date _____

Class observed and grade _____

ACTIVITY 3.2. Observation Analysis Questions

1. After reviewing your observation notes, record in the table on the next page each instance of student problem behavior you saw and the teacher's response. Also, categorize each student behavior as I (inattentive), O (off-task), or D (disruptive) and each teacher response as L (limited) or M (major).

2. Did student misbehavior occur more often during certain activities than during others? Did the teacher respond differently during different activites?

3. To what extent was the flow of activities smooth and uninterrupted? What teacher behavior and activities contributed to this flow? If interruptions occurred, how was student behavior affected?

Teacher Strategies

Code	Description

Student Behaviors

Code	Description

4. What other preventive strategies were used by the teacher? Describe how they affected student behavior.

5. Which approaches to handling student behaviors seemed most effective? For which behaviors? Which strategies are you likely to use yourself, and which would you probably not use? Why? What other approaches might be effective?

ACTIVITY 3.3. Further Questions

If you have had the opportunity to interview the teacher about managing student behavior (see Appendix A for suggested interview questions), the following questions can be answered:

1. What are the teacher's goals and philosophy regarding student discipline?

2. What schoolwide standards for behavior or approaches to discipline were mentioned by the teacher as having an impact on this class?

3. How did this teacher convey behavior expectations to the students? Has behavior changed since the beginning of school?

4. What system of incentives and penalties is used in this class? How did the teacher develop this system?

5. What type of behavior problems and strategies for dealing with them were noted by the teacher?

AREA 4
Managing Instructional Activities

Observing classroom management requires attention not only to classroom routines and behavior management but also to how teachers organize and conduct instructional activities. These different aspects of classroom management and teaching are closely linked. Pacing presentations and activities, clearly communicating content and assignments, and monitoring student understanding and completion of work all directly affect the teacher's ability to keep students successfully engaged in learning activities and prevent the boredom, frustration, and confusion that lead to management problems. In this chapter we will focus first on the organization of classroom activities and management of student assignments and then on some of the management skills involved in conducting interactive instruction.

MANAGING TIME AND ACTIVITIES

Time Use

One way to examine the management of instructional activities is to consider how class time is allocated. When planning lessons and conducting class the teacher makes many decisions about how much of the school day or hour is to be used on different topics and types of activities. For most beginning teachers, predicting how much time should be allocated for specific activities is difficult. As an observer, an awareness of time as a dimension of classroom management will help you cope with this challenging teaching task.

Teachers' decisions about time and activities are critical for several reasons. Studies have shown that time on task can be an important factor in students' learning. Of course, allocated time is usually quite different from the amount of time individual students actually spend engaged in instructional activities. For example, of the forty-five minutes a teacher might allocate for a mathematics lesson, six or more minutes may be taken up by transitions, including the time it takes to change from the preceding activity to the mathematics lesson (e.g., to get supplies and sharpen pencils), to shift activity within the lesson (e.g., to move from a teacher presentation to an independent practice assignment), and to end the lesson (e.g., to submit papers and put supplies away). In some classrooms long transitions are common; in others they are usually quick and efficient. It is important to note what the teacher does during transitions, how directions and expectations for student behavior are communicated, and how routines may reduce the need for directions.

As you have probably noticed, time on task for individual students also varies because of off-task behavior. Daydreaming, socializing, wandering, and other off-task behaviors consume significant amounts of time for some students. Another category of time use is dead time, when students have completed assigned activities and are simply waiting. Dead time can be reduced through careful planning and by providing enrichment activities, extra credit assignments, or learning centers and a set of procedures for their use.

Organization of Work

Another important component of the organization of class time and activities is what students do when they are on task. Consider format—how students are grouped for work. A common format is large-group, teacher-led instruction in which all the class is engaged in the same activity. Another is small-group instruction in which the teacher works actively with one small group (e.g., a reading group) while the others work on seat work. Still another format is cooperative work groups in which small groups work together while the teacher monitors and assists as needed.

These situations place different management demands on the teacher. For example, during a whole-class, teacher-directed activity it may be relatively easy for the teacher to watch all the students at once and notice off-task behavior. However, during large-group instruction minor misbehaviors such as inappropriate comments are public events and can easily interrupt the lesson if they persist. Although small group work is complex to organize and manage, it minimizes public confrontations and the spread of disruption or distraction. When you are observing, watch for ways that different work formats affect student and teacher behavior.

Student Assignments

Next consider the management of student assignments. Major considerations in this area are how the teacher ensures that students know what their assignments are, understand the requirements and objectives, and successfully complete the work. An important part of classroom management is the teacher's accountability system for students' work, that is, all of the procedures used to communicate assignments, monitor and keep account of student progress, and give feedback to students about their work.

Understanding classroom management also requires attention to the *content* of class work, particularly the cognitive demands of assignments, or the mental operations students must use to accomplish their work. Many assignments, such as spelling or vocabulary exercises, require students to recognize, copy, or remember information. For others students have to use routines or formulas such as those involved in mathematics or grammar. Other work may demand that students make inferences or interpretations, draw conclusions, generate and express ideas, or solve problems. Some assignments may also use complex procedures involving several steps, many details, or complex equipment.

These various types of academic work provide students with opportunities to practice different kinds of operations, but they also present different management problems for teachers. Assignments that are routine, familiar, or procedurally and cognitively simple for students are likely to be relatively easy to manage. Students usually understand what they are supposed to do, and classes are likely to proceed rather smoothly (of course, boredom and lack of motivation may also create problems). In contrast, when assignments involve new, cognitively demanding, or procedurally complex material, the teacher's job of managing students' work can become more complicated. Students may have more trouble understanding what they are to do and getting started. There may be complaints or many requests for assistance. Monitoring the class, explaining directions and objectives, encouraging students to attempt the work, and grading and giving feedback all require special attention in these circumstances. Therefore, when you observe a class, consider the kind of work students are assigned.

Adjusting Instruction

Because every class is made up of students with different abilities, interests, and knowledge, planning and adjusting activities to meet the various needs is a central management issue. Among the strategies teachers use to address this problem are small-group work, individualized instruction or assignments, enrichment or extra credit assignments, peer tutoring, learning centers, and independent projects, along with such general tactics as providing a variety of activities and changes in pace. An important consideration here is how the teacher monitors individual student progress and understanding. Some teachers learn a great deal about student performance daily by examining written assignments and quizzes, inspecting each student's work during class, and questioning and observing students. Being constantly aware of every student's comprehension and progress is very difficult (particularly in secondary schools, where teachers typically have at least 125 students), but maintaining awareness and making necessary adjustments are critical dimensions of teaching and classroom management that merit attention during field experiences.

OBSERVATION GUIDE 4.   Managing Instructional Activities

ACTIVITY 4.1.   Observe and Take Notes

Take detailed notes of class activities, focusing on how the teacher organizes instructional activities and monitors the students' work. Record details and events relating to

> format and work groupings
> student behavior and attention during different activities
> cognitive demands and procedural complexity of assignments
> introductions and directions for activities
> teacher assistance with and monitoring of student work and comprehension
> grading and checking of work
> comments about accountability
> differentiation or adjustments of activities for various students

Use the following guidelines:

1. Make a note of the time whenever there is a change in whole class or small-group activities.
2. At least every ten minutes scan the room and keep simple counts of the number of students who are off task or in dead time.
3. Select two target students, one high achiever and one lower achiever (ask your teacher for nominations, if necessary). Make frequent notes of their activities. Note especially their placement in the room, their participation and attention during different activities, their assignments and work completion, teacher assistance with and monitoring of their work, and their other interactions with the teacher and students.

ACTIVITY 4.2. Observation Analysis Questions

Use your notes to answer the following questions as soon as possible after your observation:

1. Briefly list the activities observed, in the sequence in which they occurred, noting the time, format, and topic. For example:

    4 min.   Whole class review on analogies
   16 min.   Small-group work generating analogies with chapter terms

2. Describe and give examples of the cognitive demand and procedural complexity of instructional activities for the students.

3. Describe any differences you noted in student behaviors or management demands on the teacher during various activities.

4. What, if anything, did this teacher do to adjust instruction or activities to meet the needs of the students with different abilities, achievement levels, interests, and the like? What evidence was there that such adjustment was necessary?

5. Describe any differences you noted between your two target students in their classroom behavior, assignments, participation, and interactions with the teacher.

6. Describe how this teacher collected information about student understanding and performance. By the end of the observation period, how much information did the teacher have about individual performances? Was more information obtained about some students than others?

7. Describe this teacher's system for making assignments and collecting work. Did the students seem to be aware of the requirements? Are they held accountable for their work?

ACTIVITY 4.3. Further Questions

If you have had an opportunity to interview the teacher about managing instructional activities (see Appendix A for suggested interview questions), the following questions can be answered:

1. What special management considerations or problems are associated with teaching this particular subject or grade level?

2. Describe how this teacher checks or grades daily work, including the policy and beliefs regarding late or missing assignments.

3. How did the teacher describe the range of achievement levels in the class? What strategies were reported for adjusting instruction for different students?

4. Describe the grading system used by the teacher. How are different assignments or activities counted toward a grade for a major marking period?

5. What aspects of this teacher's system for organizing activities and managing student work would you be most likely to retain in your own teaching? Which would you modify? Explain.

MANAGING INTERACTIVE INSTRUCTION

In your preceding observation you were asked to consider how different classroom activities and student assignments make various management demands on the teacher. This section takes a closer look at management of a common and very important activity—large-group, interactive instruction. This activity, which may be thought of as teaching a lesson, actually encompasses several teaching functions. One is content development, in which the teacher presents information, defines concepts, and gives explanations, examples, illustrations, and demonstrations. Through questioning and encouraging student questions and comments, the teacher also involves students in this phase of lessons. A second, overlapping function is providing guided practice and checking student understanding as the teacher questions or leads students through brief written exercises and then gives them feedback on their responses. Yet another teaching function during interactive instruction is class discussion, or the open-ended exploration of student ideas and opinions on a topic, in which the teacher encourages students to express their own beliefs and experiences and consider other points of view. Of course, all three of these functions can be conducted in small groups, but because large-group interactive instruction is very common, we will focus on such lessons in this section.

Important Concepts for This Observation

From a classroom management perspective, teacher goals in conducting interactive instruction include maintaining the clarity, flow, and focus of the lesson, engaging the attention and participation of all students, and appropriately pacing instruction to promote student comprehension.

Lesson Clarity, Flow, and Focus

Providing coherent and clear presentations of content requires careful planning of lessons, skill in directing student attention to main ideas, and care in avoiding digressions and distractions. The teacher must also use vocabulary the students will understand and systematically define new words.

As you observe instruction, notice how the teacher calls attention to lesson objectives or important ideas. Are any relationships indicated between the new content and previous lessons or assignments? Presenting step-by-step instruction and providing outlines, diagrams, or other visual props, demonstrations, and examples likewise help lessons progress smoothly.

You may notice that student comments and answers to questions during content development can affect lesson flow and clarity. Some student responses may introduce material that does not fit with the teacher's plans. Too many incorrect responses, off-the-point student questions and divergent contributions can result in a confusing presentation. Off-task student behavior and teacher responses to it can also detract from the lesson focus and flow of ideas. Notice what strategies the teacher uses to avoid distractions and steer or redirect students' attention to important content.

Student Engagement

A second critical goal for teachers during whole class lessons is to keep all the students actively engaged. One consideration is the lesson itself, for students are more likely to be engaged by lessons that are interesting, thought provoking, and filled with examples and illustrations that help them see the relevance and usefulness of the content. Other considerations are accountability and participation opportunities. Questioning students during lessons is a way of holding them accountable for paying attention. When teachers call on very few students, respond only to those volunteering answers, or answer their own questions, accountability is low. Calling on individual students for responses and distributing response opportunities widely around the class in an unpredictable pattern create greater student accountability, gives more students the opportunity to be active participants, and provides the teacher a more accurate picture of class comprehension. Requiring students to take notes (helping when necessary), occasionally asking for choral responses, and inserting short, written practice opportunities in the lesson are other ways that the teacher can increase student accountability and involvement. When you observe a class try to note such patterns of student engagement.

How the teacher communicates expectations for student behavior during interactive instruction should also be noted. Are expectations made explicit, are they governed by established routines, or are they unclear in some areas? Are students told what they should have on their desks? How does the teacher indicate what notes students are to take or what rules they are to follow for oral participation? If you have the opportunity to observe a discussion session rather than a content development lesson, notice how the different goals and expectations for this activity are communicated.

Pacing

During interactive instruction, pacing—adjusting the rate of presentation of information to the students' ability to comprehend and assimilate it—is a central problem. Because students have different levels of ability and achievement, no lesson will be perfectly paced for all students in a large group. Teachers' pacing decisions usually involve compromises. In many classes a relatively small group of students has a lot of influence on the pace of presentations. Characteristics of the students who fill this *steering group* function vary among classes, however, and some teachers are more responsive than others to such student influence. An interesting exercise when observing a class is to try to notice whether certain students are setting or influencing the pace of instruction. Does the teacher consistently check with certain individuals before proceding from one point to the next? Or does the pace seem to be influenced by one or more students who persistently ask questions, request more information, or volunteer many comments?

At the heart of the pacing problem is the teacher's awareness of student comprehension of the content during interactive instruction, for informed decisions about pacing cannot be made without such information. Active student participation—whether in the form of responses to teacher questions, volunteered questions and comments, or answers to brief practice exercises—provides crucial information to the teacher during lessons. Students' facial expressions also offer visual clues about comprehension. In addition, student performance on previous, related assignments helps the teacher anticipate problems with comprehension.

A common problem in monitoring student comprehension is that in large classes teachers tend to interact more often with (and thus obtain more information about) some students than others. For example, students seated near the teacher are more easily monitored and encouraged to participate, while those at the periphery or back of the room are sometimes seldom called on. Higher-achieving students, physically attractive or very verbal students, and those who require frequent teacher attention to stay on task may also receive more response opportunities than other students.

Such unequal patterns of participation can affect the pacing, quantity, and quality of instruction that all students receive. It also influences student accountability for their participation, their attention and comprehension, and their self-concepts. Some teachers use a variety of systems to distribute response opportunities evenly, such as patterned turns, calling names from the class roster or a stack of shuffled name cards, or (in an elementary classroom) asking for responses from students wearing clothing of a certain color. Teacher movement around the room also encourages wider student involvement and permits better monitoring. When you are observing a lesson, note how the teacher monitors comprehension and influences student participation.

ACTIVITY 4.4. Analyzing Patterns of Participation
in an Interactive Lesson

A record of student participation and behavior during a lesson presentation or discussion is useful for analyzing how the teacher influences student involvement, monitors comprehension, and adjusts the pace of instruction. An easy way to keep track of student participation is to use a seating chart or grid with simple symbols for different kinds of involvement. This system is particularly well suited to a study of classroom management because information is preserved about individual students and their positions in the room in relation to the teacher and other students.

Figure 4-1 is a sample Student Participation Survey that records student involvement during a lesson on food chains in a sixth-grade science class. During the sixteen minutes in which the teacher explained and discussed new content and questioned the students, the observer recorded student involvement using the symbols listed. When a student volunteered an answer to a teacher question either by calling out an answer or by raising a hand and being called on, a V was recorded. If the answer was incorrect, thereby showing poor student understanding, the symbol was underlined. If the teacher called on a student who had not volunteered, the response was coded as NV or NV, if incorrect. Student task-related questions or comments were noted as Q or C if directed to the teacher or as QS or CS if directed to another student. When the teacher directed a question to the class as a whole and many students called out a response, this response was marked with a check at the side. If, however, relatively few students answered and the observer could note the identities of those students, their responses were coded as V. When the teacher directed all students to complete a short written exercise during the lesson and she circulated to look at their work, note was made in the "Guided Practice" column. Students whom the teacher helped or checked during practice were coded as H. When a student was noticed off task, an O was recorded. If the behavior persisted or recurred, one or more underlines (O or O) were added.

After examining Figure 4-1, discuss what patterns of student involvement and teacher behaviors it suggests. You might want to consider:

1. How much active (verbal) student involvement occurred? (Consider the length and goal of the lesson.)
2. Which students were more actively involved? Which were less actively involved? Where were these students in the room?
3. How much off-task behavior existed? Where did it occur?
4. Which students were not successful in answering the teacher's questions?
5. Based on students' ability to answer the teacher's questions, can you infer anything about the pace of her presentation?
6. About which students' performance and understanding did the teacher gather the most information? The least?
7. What evidence exists about the teacher's position or path of movement about the room?
8. What kinds of information about questioning and lesson presentation behaviors are *not* captured in this survey?

Class _Ms. Brown's 6th Gr. General Science_

Lesson Topic/Goal _Food Chains_

Beginning Time _9:05 a.m._   Ending Time _9:21 a.m._

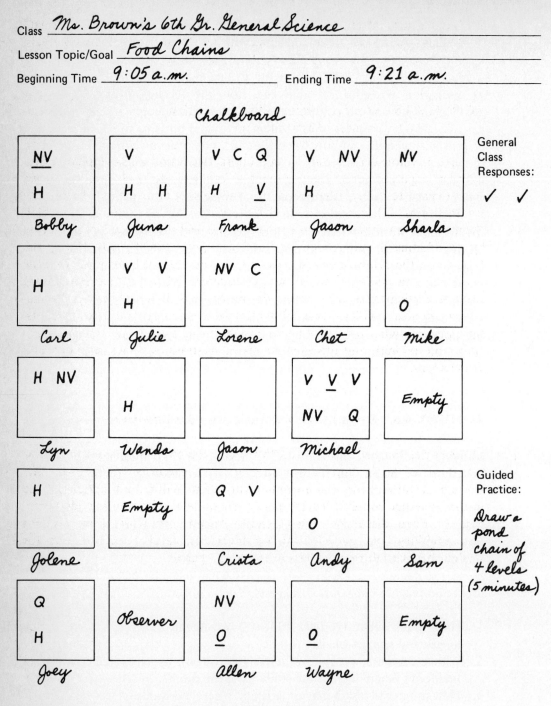

V = Student volunteers an answer (V̲ = incorrect answer)
NV = Student, nonvolunteer, answers a question (N̲V̲ = incorrect answer)
Q = Student volunteers a question of teacher (QS = of another student)
C = Student volunteers a comment to teacher (CS = to another student)
H = Teacher helps or inspects work during guided practice
O = Student off task briefly (less than 2 minutes)
O̲ or O̲ = off task repeatedly or steadily

FIGURE 4-1. Sample Student Participation Survey

9. What other patterns of participation are likely in a whole class format? Discuss their advantages and disadvantages. What types of lessons, goals, and students might make other patterns desirable?

ACTIVITY 4.5. Observing Patterns of Participation
                  in an Interactive Lesson

Observe a whole-class or large-group interactive lesson and complete a Student Participation Survey using either the form provided as Figure 4-2 or one you prepare to reflect the group size and seating arrangement. Before the lesson begins, fill in the seating chart, noting student names (if possible), vacant seats, and the positions of the observer and the teacher's presentation area (including the chalkboard and overhead projector, if used). During the lesson, use the symbols or codes listed to record student behaviors. Note the beginning and ending time of the presentation. When you are not coding student participation, also make brief notes about how the teacher emphasizes main ideas and lesson objectives; introduces and explains new concepts; tells students what behaviors are expected during the lesson (e.g., participation, note taking); and provides examples, illustrations, demonstrations, and visual props.

ACTIVITY 4.6. Summarizing and Analyzing Your Observation

Write a brief analysis of the interactive lesson you observed, paying particular attention to the student participation patterns suggested by questions one through six in Activity 4.4. Include information about the functions of the lesson, whether content development (new or review material), guided practice, or open discussion. Also describe lesson clarity and flow, student accountability and participation opportunities, teacher expectations for student behavior during the lesson, and lesson pacing.

Class _____

Lesson Topic/Goal _____

Beginning Time _____ Ending Time _____

General
Class
Responses:

Guided
Practice:

V = Student volunteers an answer (<u>V</u> = incorrect answer)
NV = Student, nonvolunteer, answers a question (<u>NV</u> = incorrect answer)
Q = Student volunteers a question of teacher (QS = of another student)
C = Student volunteers a comment to teacher (CS = to another student)
H = Teacher helps or inspects work during guided practice
O = Student off task briefly (less than 2 minutes)
<u>O</u> or O̲ = off task repeatedly or steadily

FIGURE 4-2. Student Participation Survey

APPENDIX A
Teacher Interview Questions

BACKGROUND OF THE TEACHER AND SCHOOL

1. How many years have you taught?
2. How much experience have you had teaching this grade level and/or subject?
3. How many years have you taught at this school?
4. How would you describe the community from which these students come?

AREA 1. THE CLASSROOM SETTING

1. Has your classroom been arranged this way since the beginning of the year? If not, what other arrangements have you used?
2. What do you consider when organizing classroom space?
3. How do you determine seating arrangements for individual students? How often are they changed?
4. How do you keep the papers from your different classes or subject areas separated and organized?
5. What aspects of the room, furniture, equipment, and so on do you like? Do some features cause you a problem?

AREA 2. CLASSROOM PROCEDURES AND ROUTINES

1. How did you choose the set of procedures and routines that are followed in your class? (You may want to ask about specific aspects of rules and routines listed on Observation Guide 2.)
2. How did you introduce the school and classroom procedures and routines to your students and get the students to follow them?
3. Have you made any major changes in rules or routines since the beginning of this school year? If so, please describe them and your reason for making them.
4. Are there any areas of classroom procedures or routines that you feel are particularly important or complex for a new teacher? If so, what are your recommendations regarding them?

AREA 3. MANAGING STUDENT BEHAVIOR

1. Would you say that student behavior in the class I most recently observed was typical?
2. What are your goals for student behavior or discipline?
3. What are the schoolwide behavior rules or standards? Do they affect what you do in this class?
4. How did you teach your students to behave as they do? What did you do at the beginning of the school year? How has student behavior changed since the first weeks of school?
5. What kind of penalties and rewards do you use for student behavior? How did you choose this system?
6. What behavior problems are typical for this age and grade level? What can be done to prevent or reduce the problems?
7. Do some students present more problems than others? If so, what are these problems? How do you deal with them?

AREA 4. MANAGING INSTRUCTIONAL ACTIVITIES

1. Were the kinds and sequence of instructional activities that I observed rather typical for your class? If not, what are the common patterns?
2. Are there special management considerations or problems in teaching this subject area or grade level (e.g., certain activities that require complex management)?
3. How do you check or grade daily work?
4. What is your policy regarding late or missing assignments?
5. What is the range of achievement levels in this class? Do you adjust activities or assignments for the faster and slower students? If so, how?
6. How do you determine a student's grade for a major marking period? How do different kinds of assignments (e.g., homework, tests, and projects) count toward the grade?
7. How do you plan activities for a particular class? What things do you consider?